101 Facts About

PREDATORS

101 Facts About

101 FACTS ABOUT

EAGLES

Julia Barnes

Gareth Stevens Publishing
A WORLD ALMANAC EDUCATION GROUP COMPANY

Please visit our web site at: www.garethstevens.com
For a free color catalog describing Gareth Stevens Publishing's
list of high-quality books and multimedia programs,
call 1-800-542-2595 (USA) or 1-800-387-3178 (Canada).
Gareth Stevens Publishing's fax: (414) 332-3567.

Library of Congress Cataloging-in-Publication Data available upon request from publisher.
Fax (414) 336-0157 for the attention of the Publishing Records Department.

ISBN 0-8368-4036-4

This North American edition first published in 2004 by
Gareth Stevens Publishing
A World Almanac Education Group Company
330 West Olive Street, Suite 100
Milwaukee, WI 53212 USA

This U.S. edition copyright © 2004 by Gareth Stevens, Inc. Original edition © 2003 by First
Stone Publishing. First published in 2003 by First Stone Publishing, 4/5 The Marina,
Harbour Road, Lydney, Gloucestershire, GL15 5ET, United Kingdom. Additional end
matter © 2004 by Gareth Stevens, Inc.

First Stone Series Editor: Claire Horton-Bussey
First Stone Designer: Sarah Williams
Geographical consultant: Miles Ellison
Gareth Stevens Editor: Catherine Gardner

Printed in Hong Kong through Printworks Int. Ltd.

1 2 3 4 5 6 7 8 9 08 07 06 05 04

WHAT IS A PREDATOR?

Predators are nature's hunters – the creatures that must kill in order to survive. They come in all shapes and sizes, ranging from the mighty lion to a slithering snake.

Although predators are different in many ways, they do have some things in common. All predators are necessary in the balance of nature. Predators control the number of other animals, preventing disease and starvation. In addition, all predators adapted, or changed, to survive where they live. They developed special skills to find **prey** and kill it in the quickest, simplest way possible.

The mighty eagle soars above Earth and patrols the ground below. When it finds prey, it dives with deadly precision.

101 Facts About EAGLES

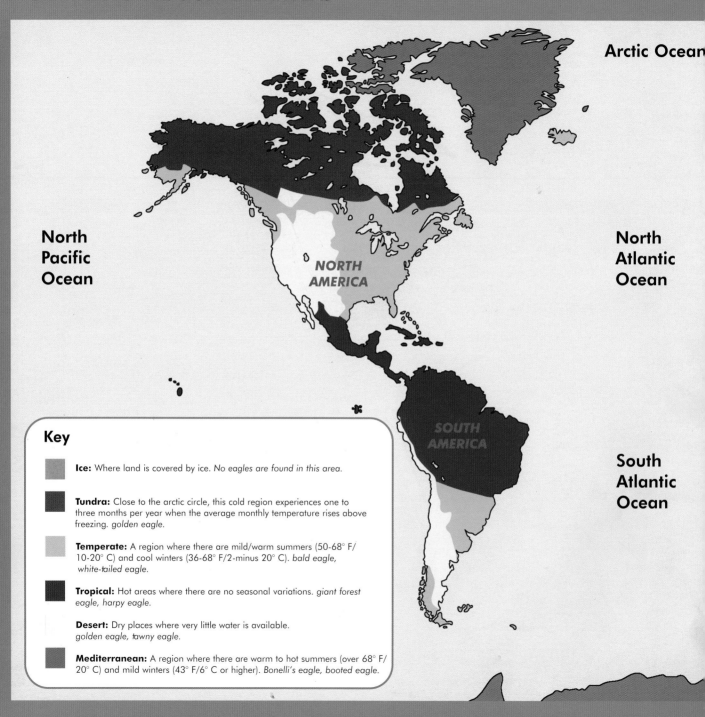

Arctic Ocean

North Pacific Ocean

North Atlantic Ocean

NORTH AMERICA

South Atlantic Ocean

SOUTH AMERICA

Key

Ice: Where land is covered by ice. *No eagles are found in this area.*

Tundra: Close to the arctic circle, this cold region experiences one to three months per year when the average monthly temperature rises above freezing. *golden eagle.*

Temperate: A region where there are mild/warm summers (50-68° F/ 10-20° C) and cool winters (36-68° F/2-minus 20° C). *bald eagle, white-tailed eagle.*

Tropical: Hot areas where there are no seasonal variations. *giant forest eagle, harpy eagle.*

Desert: Dry places where very little water is available. *golden eagle, tawny eagle.*

Mediterranean: A region where there are warm to hot summers (over 68° F/ 20° C) and mild winters (43° F/6° C or higher). *Bonelli's eagle, booted eagle.*

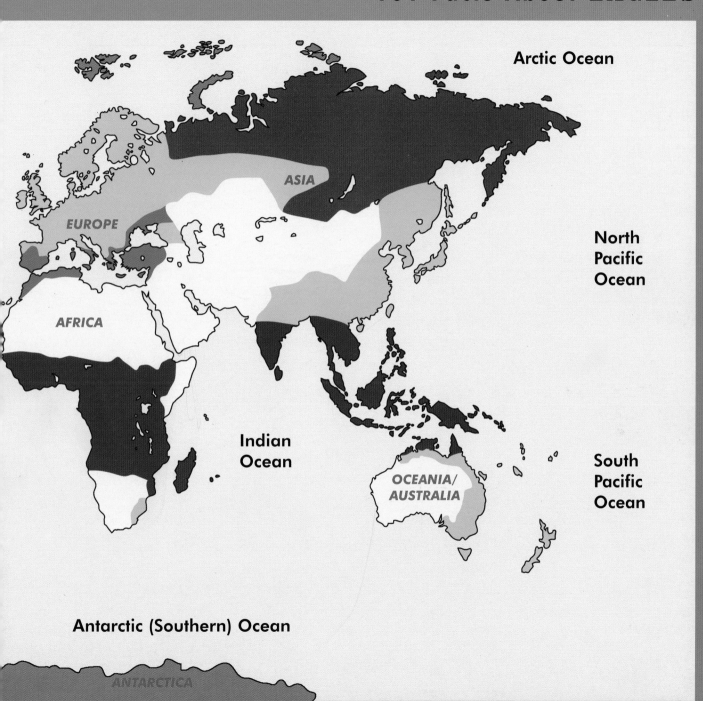

Arctic Ocean

ASIA

EUROPE

North
Pacific
Ocean

AFRICA

Indian
Ocean

OCEANIA/
AUSTRALIA

South
Pacific
Ocean

Antarctic (Southern) Ocean

ANTARCTICA

1 Eagles, hawks, falcons, and even vultures and buzzards are birds of prey. Birds of prey, called **raptors**, hunt other animals for food.

2 Birds of prey are superb hunters. They have keen eyesight, curved **talons**, and sharp bills, or beaks. Their strong wings help them soar (below).

3 Between thirty million and fifty million years ago, birds of prey began to take shape on Earth. They developed in different ways.

4 Eagles are some of the biggest and best-known of all birds of prey. Today, they live on every continent except Antarctica (see pages 4-5) and in many different kinds of climates.

5 Eagles have made their homes in rain forests, mountains, open grasslands, and lake and coastal areas.

6 The biggest eagle of all is the harpy eagle from South America (right), which is about 3 feet (1 meter) in height and has a **wingspan** of 7.5 feet (2.3 m).

7 The little eagle of New Guinea and Australia is the world's smallest eagle. A full-sized little eagle grows to be 19 inches (48 centimeters) tall and weighs 2.5 pounds (1 kilogram).

8 The fifty-nine **species** of eagles are often studied as groups that have similar features. The four groups are the fish, snake, booted, and giant forest eagles.

11 Most snake eagles are smaller than the other types of eagles. Long feathers cover their heads, and their short, strong talons help them handle prey. They eat snakes, other **reptiles**, and **amphibians**.

9 Fish eagles, sometimes called sea eagles, live on the shores of lakes, near rivers, and along coastlines. Fish is their main food.

10 Fish eagles include Steller's sea eagles from eastern Asia (above) and bald eagles, which live in North America. Eleven species of eagles belong to the fish eagle group.

12 The banded snake eagle from Africa and the crested serpent eagle from southeast Asia (right) belong to the snake eagle group.

13 Thick feathers that look like boots cover the legs of all the eagles in the booted eagle group, the largest of the four groups.

14 The booted species include the golden eagle of North America and Verreaux's eagle (right) and the tawny eagle of Africa.

15 Giant forest eagles, or harpy eagles, live in the tropical rain forests of South America, Mexico, New Guinea, and the Philippines. Only six species belong to this group of eagles.

16 The species of giant tree eagles are so big that they can hunt, catch, and kill monkeys, tree sloths, and other jungle animals.

17 Each eagle species has its own colors and features. Many have different lifestyles and diets, depending on where they live. All eagles do have some things in common.

18 To hunt and catch prey, eagles depend on their amazing flying skills. They can fly long distances, soar high in the sky, make precise dives, and carry prey.

19 Most eagles have long, broad wings (above) with stiff and strong feathers. The front edges of the wings are thicker than the trailing edges, allowing air to flow faster over the top of the wings and create lift.

20 As eagles take off or fly at low levels, they must flap their wings. At higher levels, they soar on **thermals**, columns of warm air rising from the surface of Earth. The eagles only flap their wings to move from one thermal to the next.

21 A soaring eagle does not seem to move its wings at all. In fact, an eagle does make tiny adjustments in the way it holds its wings all the time. It fine-tunes the position of the feathers at its wing tips to take advantage of the changes in air flow.

22 Some eagles fly as many as 100 miles (160 kilometers) each day to find food. They may patrol a **territory** of 60 square miles (155 square km).

23 Different species of eagles have slightly different kinds of wings and tails. Their wings and tails suit their habitats.

24 Giant forest eagles, such as the harpy eagle (right), live in tropical rain forests. The giant forest eagles have shorter, more rounded wings and a longer tail than other eagles. They need to fly easily between trees and branches.

25 The broad wings and shorter tails of fish eagles give them extra lift so they can pull prey from the water.

11

26 The long wings and tiny tail of the bateleur (left) help it cruise over African grasslands. It flies for most of the day at speeds of up to 50 miles (80 km) per hour.

27 In air, the bateleur seems to somersault and do other stunts. Its name comes from the French word for acrobat.

28 To spot prey from the air, eagles need excellent eyesight. Eagles can see four to eight times better than humans.

29 An eagle soaring in the sky can spot a rabbit from as far as 2 miles (3.2 km) away.

30 Like people, eagles see much better in daylight than at night. Most eagles do not hunt after the sun goes down.

31 Eagles see a great amount of detail and adjust the **focus** of their eyes at lightning speed. They are able to keep a sharp focus as they swoop down from the sky to grab their prey.

32 Eagles have very big eyes (below) for the size of their heads. Their eyes do not move easily, so eagles must turn their heads to see to the side.

33 See-through inner eyelids let an eagle blink without closing its eyes completely.

ground at about 150 miles (240 km) per hour.

36 The speeding eagle stops its prey in its tracks. The eagle's talons hit with the force of a bullet shot from a rifle.

34 As an eagle flies, it looks for signs of a prey animal. When it sees a likely meal, it moves quickly. In seconds, it flies over the prey and dives in for the kill.

37 The talons are sharp as razors, and they are unbelievably powerful. Once an eagle has gripped its prey, the animal has little chance of escape.

35 The **stoop**, or dive, of an eagle reaches incredible speeds. A golden eagle (above) diving at its prey plunges toward the

38 The more the victim struggles, the tighter the talons take hold.

39 The talons are so well adapted for gripping that most eagles find it difficult to walk.

40 Different species of eagles have developed special talons to suit the prey they hunt.

41 Snake eagles have short, strong toes for holding onto a wriggling snake or lizard. In addition, they have tough scales on their legs to protect them from snake bites.

42 Fish eagles, such as the white-tailed eagle from Europe (below), have large, strong feet. On the bottom of their toes are small spikes to help them hold onto slippery fish.

15

43 The crowned hawk eagle from Africa (below) has short, thick toes and stiff talons for catching bigger prey.

44 The record prey of a crowned hawk eagle was a **bushbuck** that weighed 35 pounds (16 kg), which is four times as much as the eagle.

45 Once the eagle has caught its prey, it carries it to a place where it can eat without disturbance.

46 The eagle's strong, hooked bill and its powerful jaw muscles attack the prey and rip the meat into bite-sized chunks.

47 The size of the bill depends on the type of prey that the eagle eats.

Snake eagles, which often swallow their prey whole, have smaller bills.

48 The Steller's sea eagle is one of the most powerful of all birds. It lives on a diet of fish and seal pups and has a huge and powerful bill.

49 Despite the eagle's tremendous hunting skills, only about one in four attacks from the air produce a meal.

50 Flying around and searching for prey

(above) uses a lot of energy. Instead, some eagles wait for prey at a lookout point, such as a tree or a post.

51 The eagle may stay on a perch for hours without moving. It watches patiently for any sign that a mouse, rabbit, or other small mammal is near.

52 If the eagle spots prey, it must dive from its perch before the animal finds **cover**.

53 Eagles eat whatever animals are easiest to find in the areas where they live.

54 For a golden eagle (below), some of the best places to call home are mountain cliffs and ledges. Soaring on wings that span 7 feet (2 m), the golden eagle searches for prey.

55 Ground squirrels and other **rodents**, rabbits, hares, grouse, and even waterfowl are all prey to golden eagles, which are found in North America, Asia, and Europe.

56 Like many other eagles, the golden eagle eats dead animals it finds, especially in winter when food is scarce.

57 The martial eagle (right) is the largest eagle in Africa. It flies over grassy plains to hunt prey, such as small birds and mammals.

58 Big animals can be prey, too. Martial eagles attack impala calves, small antelopes, monkeys, and **hyraxes**.

59 Giant forest eagles need different skills to hunt in their tropical rain forest habitat, which is full of trees, branches, and vines.

60 The harpy lives in the treetops of the rain forest. To find a meal, it flies through dense leaves, dives between branches, and twists around trees. When a harpy flies, monkeys flee.

61 Monkeys, sloths, and other mammals are the favorite prey of the huge harpy eagle.

and swim with their wings before taking off.

64 Stealing is another way to get meals. An eagle may take another bird's kill, especially when live prey is hard to find.

62 Sometimes, eagles find an easy source of food. Many types of fish eagles pick up dead or dying fish that have just **spawned**.

65 By diving at a heron or pelican that has made a kill, an African fish eagle (left) may force the bird to drop its prey.

63 Bald eagles snatch fish from just below the surface of the water and head straight for land. Once in a while, they hit the water

66 Bald eagles attack ospreys, their main competitors for fish, so they can steal opreys' catches.

67 Hunting takes up much of the eagle's day, particularly when young eagles are sitting in the nest and waiting to be fed.

68 When they are not hunting, many kinds of eagles spend time resting on a tree branch (right).

69 Resting helps eagles save energy for the demanding work of hunting and take advantage of the best flying conditions.

70 Eagles soar on thermals created when the air temperature rises. Heavy rain or strong wind can make flying difficult.

71 The search for food forces eagles that live in colder climates to **migrate** in winter. The eagles that live in the north go south, and the eagles that live on mountains head to lower slopes.

72 Migrating eagles fly during the daytime, when the thermals help them soar, and they travel alone. Large groups of eagles often gather together in the same area for the winter months.

73 Eagles are ready to mate when they are four to five years old. Many species, including the bald eagle (left) and the golden eagle, keep the same mates for their whole lives.

74 When eagles try to select mates, they often join in amazing stunts in the air, which are called courtship displays.

75 Both the female and male usually take part in the courtship display. They may fly high in the sky, make a steep dive, and pull up at the last second. They speed toward each other, roll, and fly upside down.

76 A pair of courting African fish eagles clasps talons in midair. Then, still holding talons, they start to cartwheel downward over and over again, until they let go and pull up before hitting the ground.

77 A Verreaux's eagle (right), also called a black eagle, lives in eastern and southern Africa. It dives from heights of 1,000 feet

(305 m) with folded wings and then stretches its wings to pull out of the dive.

78 A mated pair chases other eagles away from a certain territory, or area of land. The territory size varies with different species and habitats.

79 The female chooses the site for the nest, which is known as an aerie, but both eagles build it.

80 Some eagle species build themselves a new nest every year. Other eagles repair and add new materials to the same nest year after year.

81 A bald eagle (above) holds the record for the world's biggest tree nest at 9 feet (3 m) across. Most eagle nests never reach such a record size.

82 Usually, eagles lay one to three eggs with a gap of several days between each laying.

83 Females **incubate** the eggs and guard the nest. Males are smaller and more agile, so they hunt and bring food back to the waiting females.

84 In about forty days, depending on the species, the first egg hatches. Any other eggs hatch later.

85 The young, called eaglets, are small and completely helpless at birth (right). They have soft **down** on their bodies. They do not weigh much, but their legs are too weak to stand.

86 The first eaglet that hatches has a few days to grow stronger and bigger before the rest hatch.

87 The biggest eaglet often takes the most food and may even peck at a smaller one until it dies.

88 Letting the smallest eaglet die may be a way for eagles to ensure the other young get enough food to grow strong and survive.

89 Both parents guard the nest (below) and bring food to the young. The adults shelter the eaglets from bad weather, shading them from the intense heat of the sun and covering them from heavy rain.

90 Eaglets grow up quickly. They begin to walk around in the nest, and soon, stiff adult feathers replace their fluffy down. Finally, they are ready to try out their wings (right).

91 The age an eaglet takes its first flight is different for each type of eagle. A golden eagle may be only two months old when it tries to fly for the first time.

92 A giant forest eagle, such as a harpy, is four to six months old before it is ready to fly.

93 The young eaglets stay near the area of the nest for up to one year. During their first year, they rely on their parents for some of their food while they perfect their hunting skills.

94 Some species of eagles must take care of their offspring for so long that they can only mate every other year.

95 Throughout history, eagles have been a symbol of strength for many countries. Now, the survival of some eagles is in danger.

96 People take more land for cities and for industry, and they destroy the wild places eagles and their prey need to live.

97 Humans have also killed many eagles on purpose. Some people think eagles prey on farm animals or eat too many of the fish people want for themselves (left).

98 **Pesticides**, which run from fields and lawns into lakes and rivers, poison fish. Bald eagles and other fish eagles eat the fish and die, too.

99 Bald eagles (right) numbered about 500,000 in North America in 1782, when they became

the national symbol for the United States. By the 1960s, so few bald eagles remained in the wild that some people feared they would die out.

recovering. Other species, such as the Philippine eagle, are losing the struggle with people and remain in grave danger of dying out.

100 **Conservation** work has helped to protect bald eagles from humans, and the species is

101 Without help, the mighty predator of the sky does not stand a chance against humans.

Glossary

amphibians: animals such as frogs, toads, and salamanders.

bushbuck: a small type of antelope.

conservation: the preservation and protection of something, such as natural resources.

cover: an area where a prey animal can hide.

down: soft, fluffy feathers on birds.

focus: the point of clearest vision.

hyraxes: small African animals that are related to elephants.

incubate: to keep eggs warm until they hatch.

migrate: to move with the seasons.

pesticides: chemicals used to kill insects on plants.

predators: animals that kill other animals for food.

prey: an animal a predator chooses to hunt and kill.

raptors: birds that hunt animals.

reptiles: animals such as lizards and snakes.

rodents: small, gnawing animals, such as rats, mice, and squirrels.

spawned: produced and deposited eggs in an area such as a riverbed.

species: types of animals or plants that are alike in many ways.

stoop: a steep, predatory dive.

talons: the claws of birds of prey.

territory: an area that an animal lives in and defends as its own.

thermals: columns of warm air that rise from Earth.

wingspan: length of both wings from tip to tip.

More Books to Read

**Bald Eagle Magic for Kids
(Animal Magic for Kids series)**
Charlene Gieck
(Gareth Stevens)

The Bald Eagle Returns
Dorothy Hinshaw Patent
(Houghton Mifflin)

Eagles (Buddy Book series)
Julie Murray
(ABDO)

Eagles (Zoobooks series)
John B. Wexo
(Wildlife Education)

Web Sites

Alaska Fish and Game Department
www.state.ak.us/local/akpages/FISH.
GAME/notebook/bird/eagles.htm

American Eagle Foundation
www.eagles.org/

The Big Zoo
www.thebigzoo.com/zoo/
Falconiformes.asp

Kids' Planet Fact Sheets
www.kidsplanet.org/factsheets/
bald_eagle.html

To find additional web sites, use a reliable search engine to find one or more of the following keywords: **bald eagle, bateleur eagle, raptor.**

 # Index